Easter
COLORING BOOK
FOR KIDS

AGES
4-8

CECILE
SINGLETON

CECILE SINGLETON

CECILE SINGLETON

CECILE
SINGLETON

CECILE
SINGLETON

CECILE SINGLETON

CECILE SINGLETON

CECILE
SINGLETON

CECILE
SINGLETON

CECILE SINGLETON

CECILE
SINGLETON

CECILE SINGLETON

CECILE SINGLETON

CECILE SINGLETON

CECILE SINGLETON

CECILE
SINGLETON

CECILE
SINGLETON

CECILE SINGLETON

CECILE
SINGLETON

CECILE
SINGLETON

CECILE SINGLETON

CECILE
SINGLETON

CECILE
SINGLETON

CECILE
SINGLETON

CECILE
SINGLETON

CECILE
SINGLETON

Made in the USA
Monee, IL
31 March 2021